Paper House Models 3 US Midwest House Model Patterns

Missouri, Nebraska, and North Dakota

by Denise McGill

To all the many children I have taught art lessons to using some of these house models and patterns; especially Luna, Nataly, Kevin, and Kim

CONTENTS

Missouri House MO

Nebraska Stone House NE

North Dakota Old Ranch House ND

This book is one of a series of US Paper House Models.
There are 17 books in the series divided into regions of the US:
US Northeast States
US Southern States
US Midwest States
US Western States
Collect them all and support your local artists.

Paper House Construction

Houses, houses, houses… they are everywhere. If you are like me, you like to look at all the different kinds of houses; to draw houses; to live in a house. And when a new house is built down the street, don't you like to go and watch the construction, just like me? Well, if you like houses, old and new, you will just love this project. You can make a whole town with some heavy paper, colored pencils and a little glue.

Impress your teachers, family and friends with how much you know about architecture, geometry, and mathematics. You could even add some white acrylic paint for "snow" on the roofs and create a Christmas town. Either way, you will really enjoy the process of building your own houses.

The materials you will need are:

- Heavy paper, like card stock, tag board, or watercolor paper
- House patterns
- Colored pencils or markers
- Acrylic paint optional
- Scissors and glue
- Exacto knife (optional for some patterns)
- small beads for door knobs

Now you are set to explore the town. Each house presents its own difficulty levels. It is best to start with the easiest house and build up your experience (no pun intended) in construction before tackling the more difficult ones.

Copying the pattern.

I suggest heavy paper, cover weight photocopy paper (65 or 80 lbs), tag board, or watercolor paper because these will make a good solidly constructed house. Cover weight photocopy paper is good but watercolor paper is even better. The only problem with the watercolor paper is that it cannot be put through your printer and the pattern would have to be copied onto the paper manually. White construction paper is not best because it can be crushed easily. It isn't as sturdy and strong unless you start by gluing two sheets together for a thicker paper.

Most house patterns have two pages each. Several have three pages and a few have more.

With each house, you will need to trace the patterns onto the heavy paper or print it directly onto cover weight paper. To do this, you can use carbon paper OR try a fun artist's trick.

Sometimes artists turn the pattern over and scribble over the back side with a #2 pencil, covering the back side as much as possible. What you are doing is making the pattern into "carbon paper". Then, when you trace over the pattern onto the white watercolor paper, the lines from the other side transfer to the white paper. Another trick is to hold the pattern page and heavy paper together up against a window. The light from outside the window makes it easy to see through both papers to copy the pattern. You are making your windows into a "light box". What a great trick, right? This is probably the least messy of the three methods.

Textures.

There are many texture possibilities to adorn your houses. Using several shades of reds and browns, color a brick pattern as in the illustration. The brick pattern is good for the chimney or the walls of a house.

 Red Brick

 various colored Brick

 log cabin

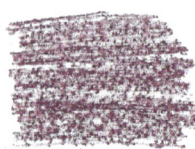 texture over sandpaper

 texture over canvas

 texture over wood

Roof texture

 Spanish tile   tar paper    wood shingle

Try a log cabin pattern. Draw little circles staggered at the corners of the house. Then color the logs.

There are several roof pattern textures. A hash pattern looks like small wood shakes. Red half circles look like adobe roof. Cross hatching looks like wood shingles. The choices are endless.

If you want your home to look vacant or abandoned, color the windows black. If you want them to look like the lights are on or candles are lit, color the windows yellow. For daylight when you don't need to turn on the lights, color the windows sky blue because glass reflects what is around like a tree or a big blue sky.

Coloring

Color the house completely, including the roof and any accessory elements like window shades, balcony, and chimney before doing the cutting. It makes it much easier to color first and cut and fold later.

Color the house any colors you like. You can make them brick buildings, red and brown or painted wood structures... as you desire. Try coloring the walls a rustic wood-brown, or go for the charming painted look with curtains in the windows.

Now it is time. Pull out your tools and begin construction.

Scoring

With heavy paper, it is necessary to score the paper to get it to fold easily. To do this you need a ruler and a blunt point of a knitting needle or a dotting tool to make a dent in the paper. Sometimes you can open a pair of scissors and use only one point. Place the ruler on the fold line

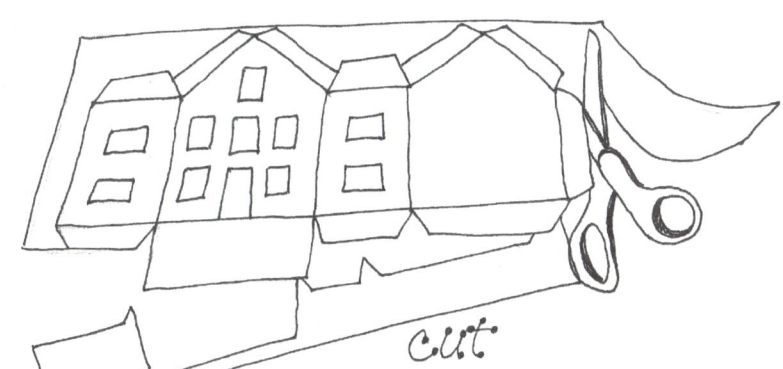

and use the point of the scissors to "draw" along the

ruler as in the diagram. Don't press too hard or you may cut the paper. Don't press too light or nothing will happen. This takes a little practice but soon you will find the perfect pressure. The point is to make a depression in the paper making it easier to fold. Large manufacturing companies have machines to do this to fold cardboard boxes but the technique is the same. Practice on a spare piece of paper until you feel confident.

The lines to score are the thin lines of the house pattern. The big bold lines are for cutting.

Cutting and Construction

When you have finished your coloring and your are

happy with the house, cut it out carefully. Make sure to cut on the bold black lines and not on the fine lines. Be very careful to include all the flaps. They will be vital in gluing the house together.

Fold all the corners of the house including the floor and the flaps for gluing. Also fold the roof in half so it will fit on the house easily. Some house roofs have extra fold lines to make the roof look more 3-dimensional.

I have a few video tutorials on my YouTube channel if you would like to see better how this is done. Check them out at: www.youtube.com/DPaintbrush.

Gluing

Using regular school white glue, start by gluing the main flap (usually marked "flap #1) to the other side of the house causing it to look more like a cylinder or a box with no top or bottom. Hold the walls gently until the glue bonds (about 20 to 30 seconds). Next glue the floor to the three floor flaps, also holding it until it sticks well.

Usually you are ready for the roof at this point. Fold the roof in half. Some roofs have extra fold lines around the edges to give the roof more of a three-dimensional quality. Fold those before placing the roof in on the house. Place the roof in position and check it

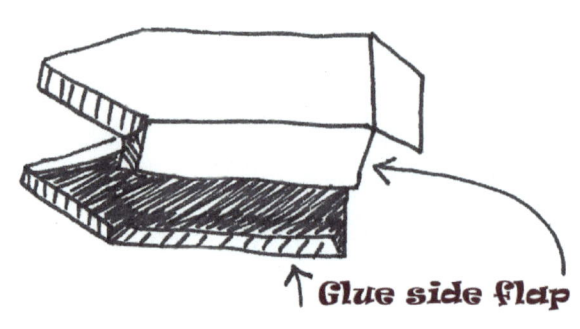
Glue side flap

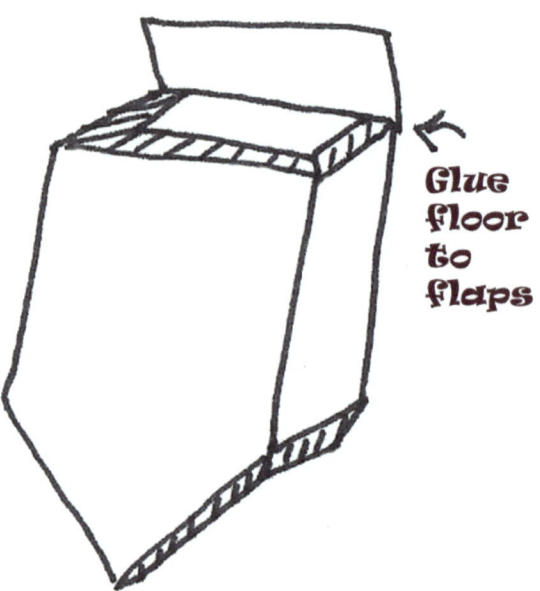
Glue floor to flaps

Glue roof to roof flaps

before gluing. When you are happy about the placement, squeeze the glue onto the folded flaps of the house then place the roof back on. Again you will have to hold it down for a few seconds until it stays in place.

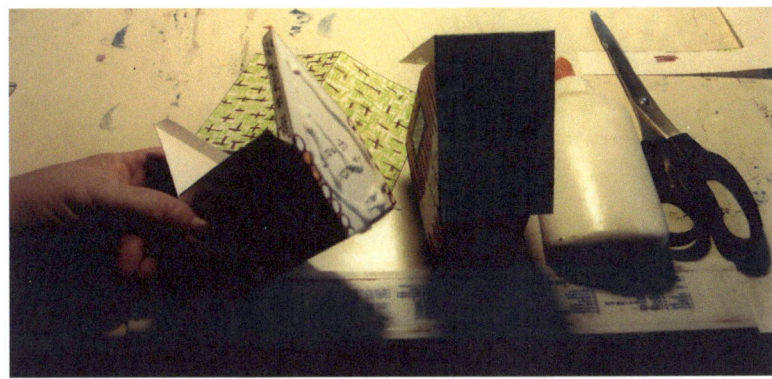

Many patterns have dormer windows, chimney, and even window shades or balconies or other accessories.

Alternate Construction

Some people like the idea of lights in the windows and snow of the roof. If you want to carefully cut out the windows and place/glue a small piece of tissue paper (white or yellow) over the inside of each window, a tea light will show through. You would want to do this before the house is glued together for ease. You can leave a trap door in the floor or just not glue the flaps to be able to place the light inside. Fun.

Another way to get a light inside would be to use Christmas twinkle lights that can be removed for storage later. Just poke a hole in the bottom of the floor for the twinkle light to go through.

Another alternate is to copy the blank house pattern and add your own details, windows, door, etc. I like to add a little wooden bead for door knobs. It is a great way to expand your ideas and creativity.

You may notice in some of the photos of the houses I have small plants and trees. I created these simple shapes using the same coloring and cutting method and left-over paper from the houses. I made a simple cylinder or conical shaped pot and then glued the thin leaves and flowers into the pot. The little tree was made by twisting wire strands together at the trunk and pulling them apart as they got further from the roots. Then I added glue to the wires and cut small pieces of green, golden yellow, orange and pink pieces of paper to the ends. This was a fun diversion for me and your students may find it so also. Experimentation is the key. Try things and if it doesn't work, try something else. Enjoy the process.

Either way, enjoy your magical village.

If you have any questions or would like more information ont he many projects I have developed, feel free to email me at dancingpaintbrush@gmail.com.

Check out my website at www.dancingpaintbrushco.com.

Many of my patterns I have constructed and recorded for YouTube videos. You can check out my YouTube tutorials at: www.youtube.com/DPaintbrush

MISSOURI FARMHOUSE

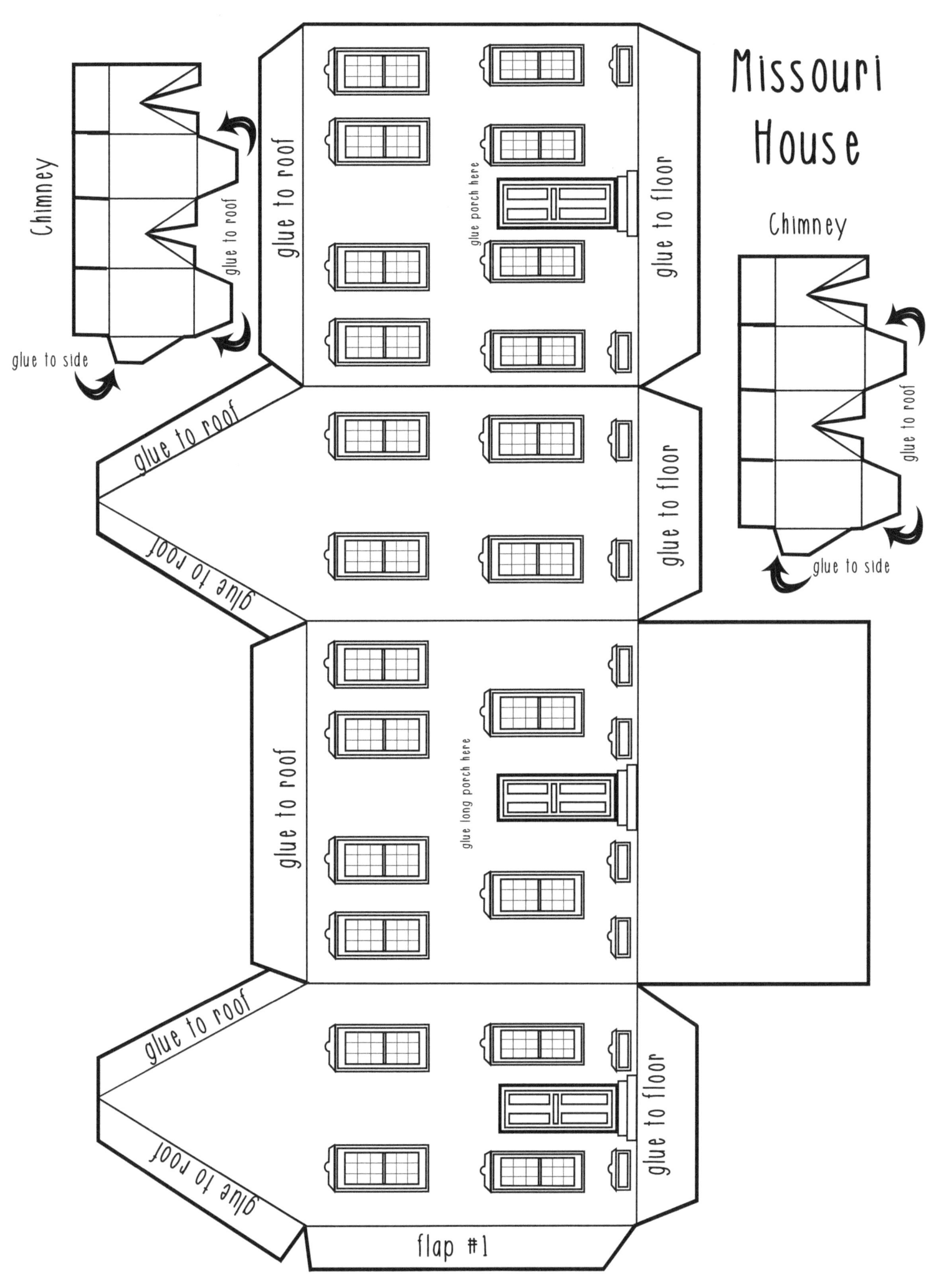

Missouri Farm House

Porch Roof

Roof

Long Porch Porch Roof

Porch Railing

Short Porch

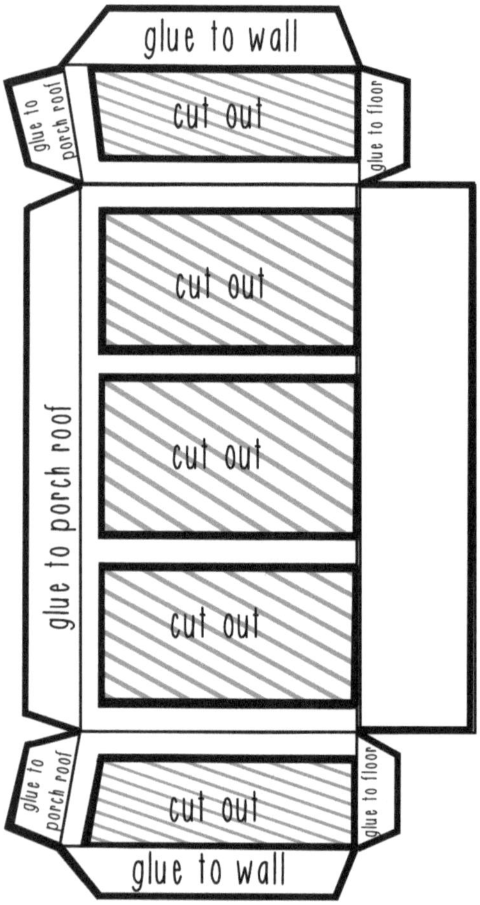

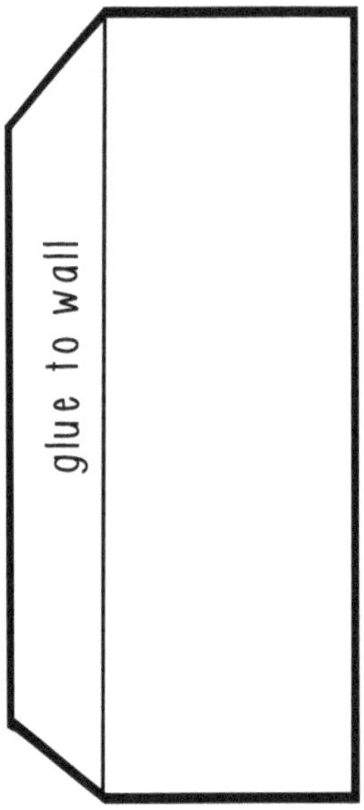

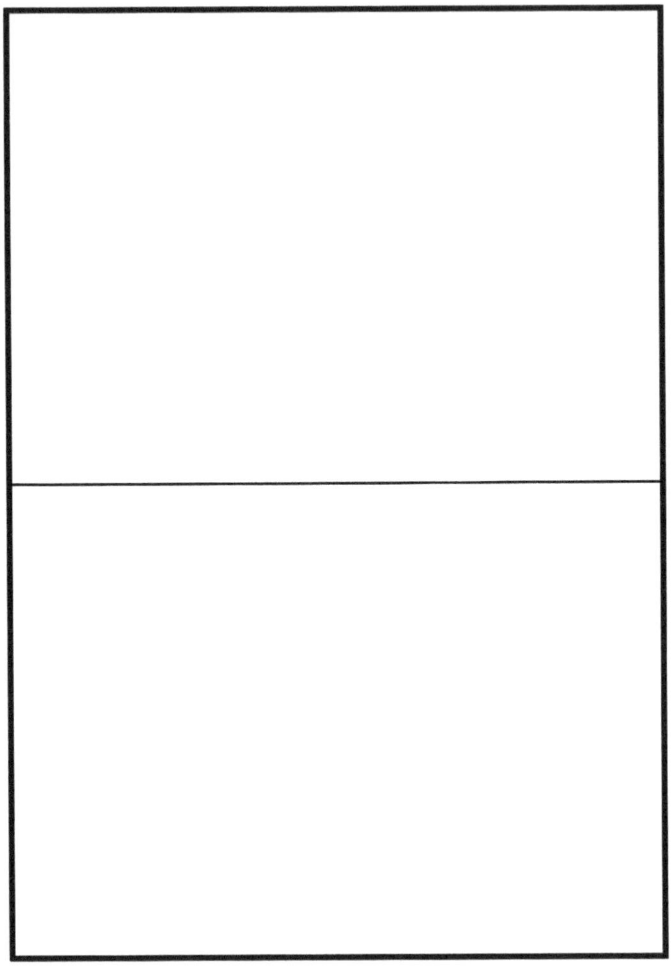

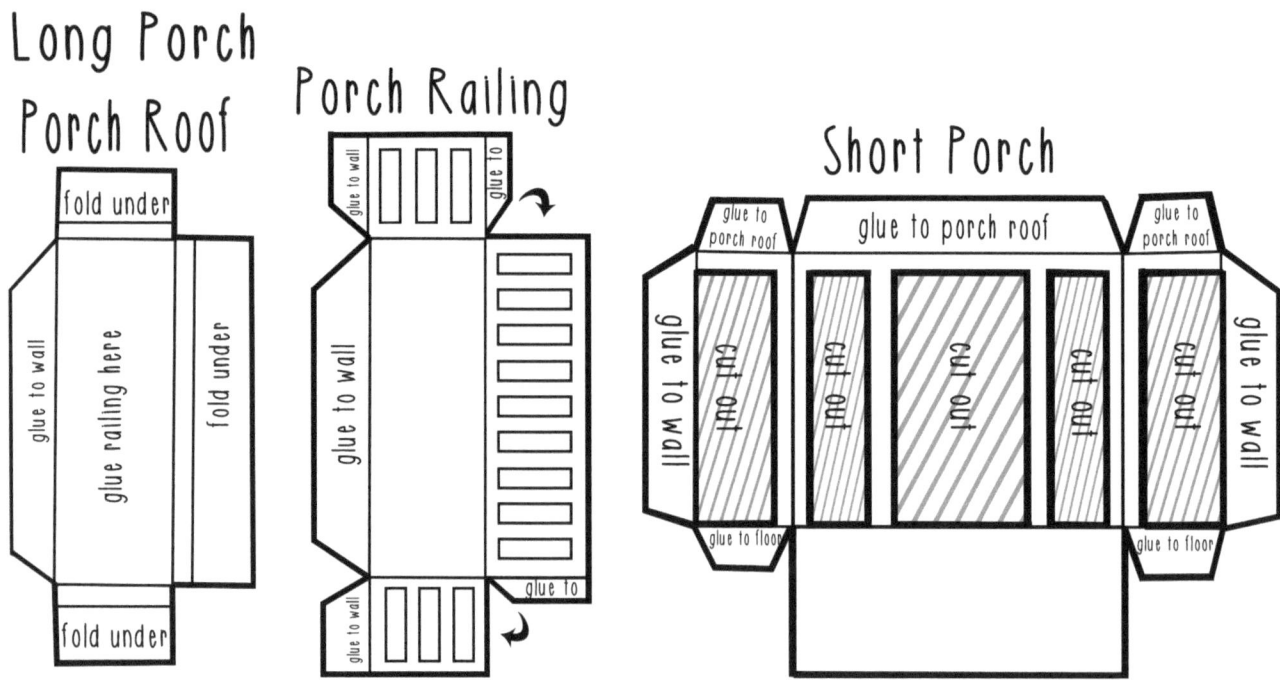

Missouri Farm House Construction

The Missouri Farmhouse doesn't have to be designed and colored like brick house but I made mine that way. The house has two porches front and back with a flat roof and railing over one and a slanted roof over the other. There are two optional chimneys as well making this an easy little compact house. The house would be great for the first grader without the porches and challenging for the 5th and 6th grade students with the porches. I have a YouTube video showing this little house's construction if you are interested to see it: https://youtu.be/GX9sFVbCWRY. The finished house measure about 6" x 4" x 4".

Construction is done in the same way as the first chapter mentions. The pages are colored as you desire. The house parts are scored and glued first and porch parts attached after the roof is glued. The porches have to have the space between rails must be cut out with a knife. On top of one of the porches is a balcony railing attached to the roof. It can be left off but I thought it added a real charm. The spaces between the railing don't have to be cut out with exacto knife or box cutter, but it looks best that way. This should be done by older students or adult supervision.

The blank pattern without windows and doors are for creative students to add their own window and door designs.

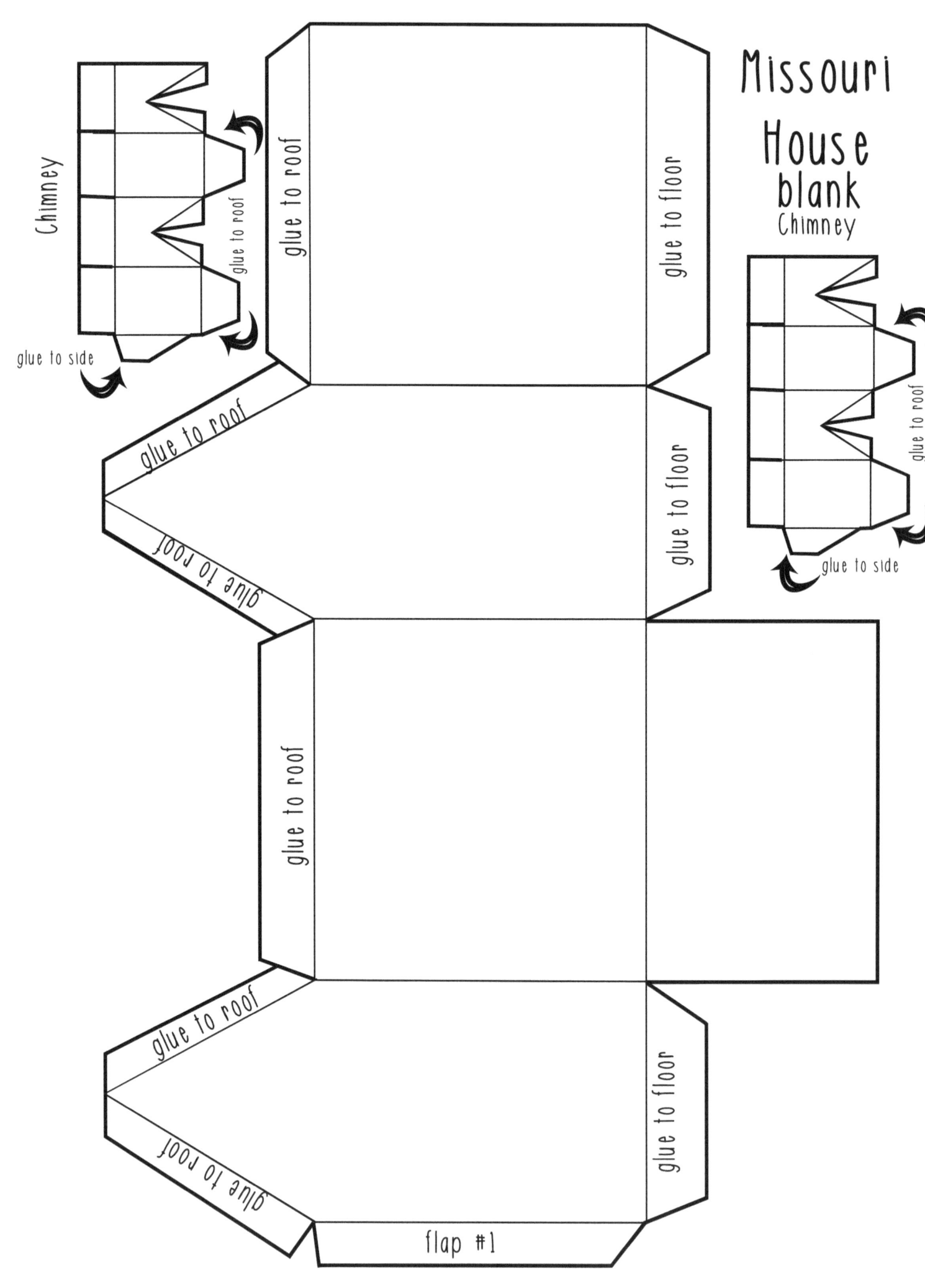

Missouri Farm House

Roof

Porch Roof

Long Porch

Porch Roof

Porch Railing

Short Porch

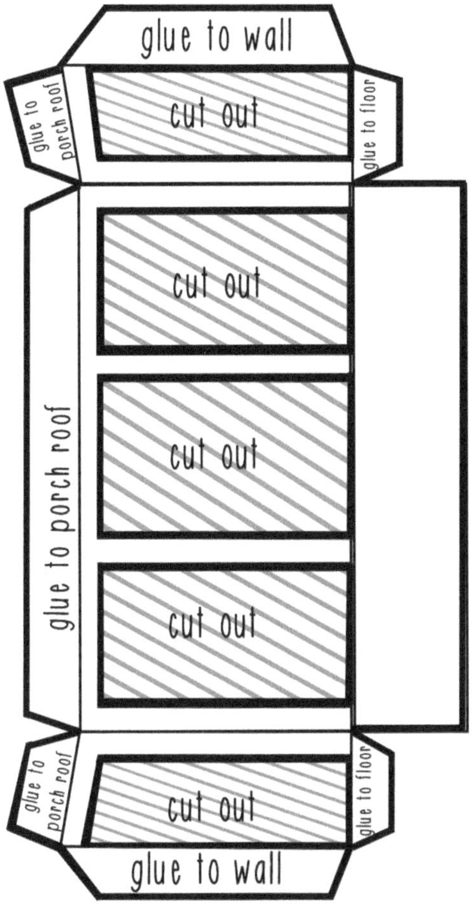

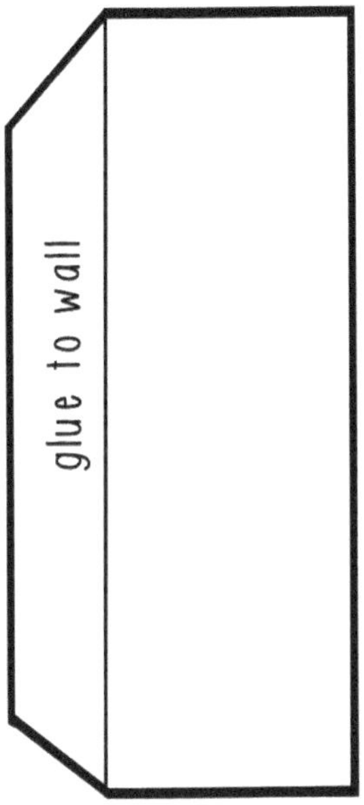

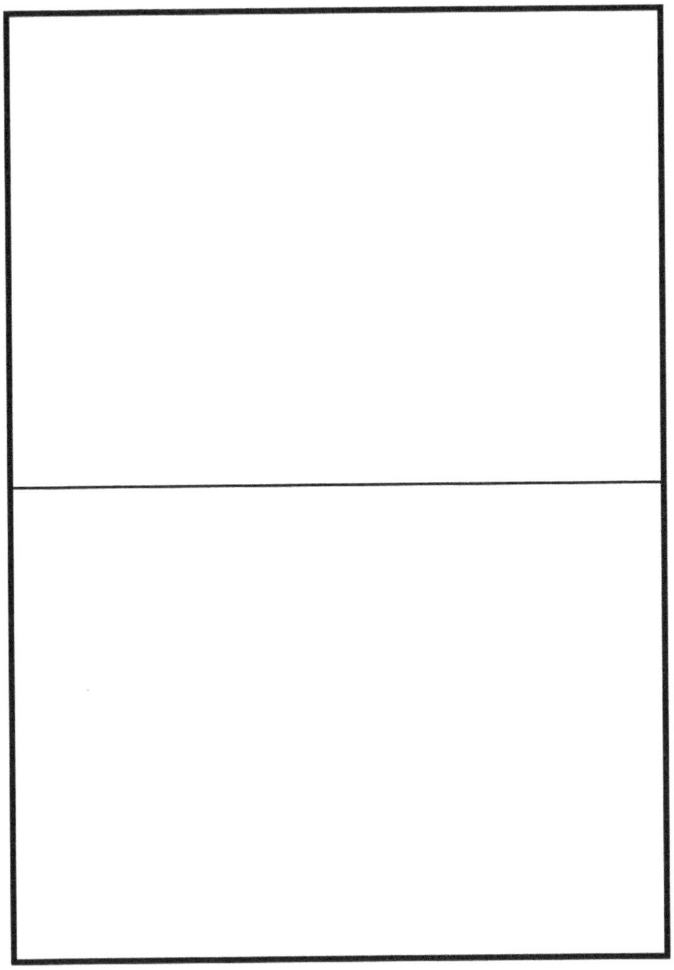

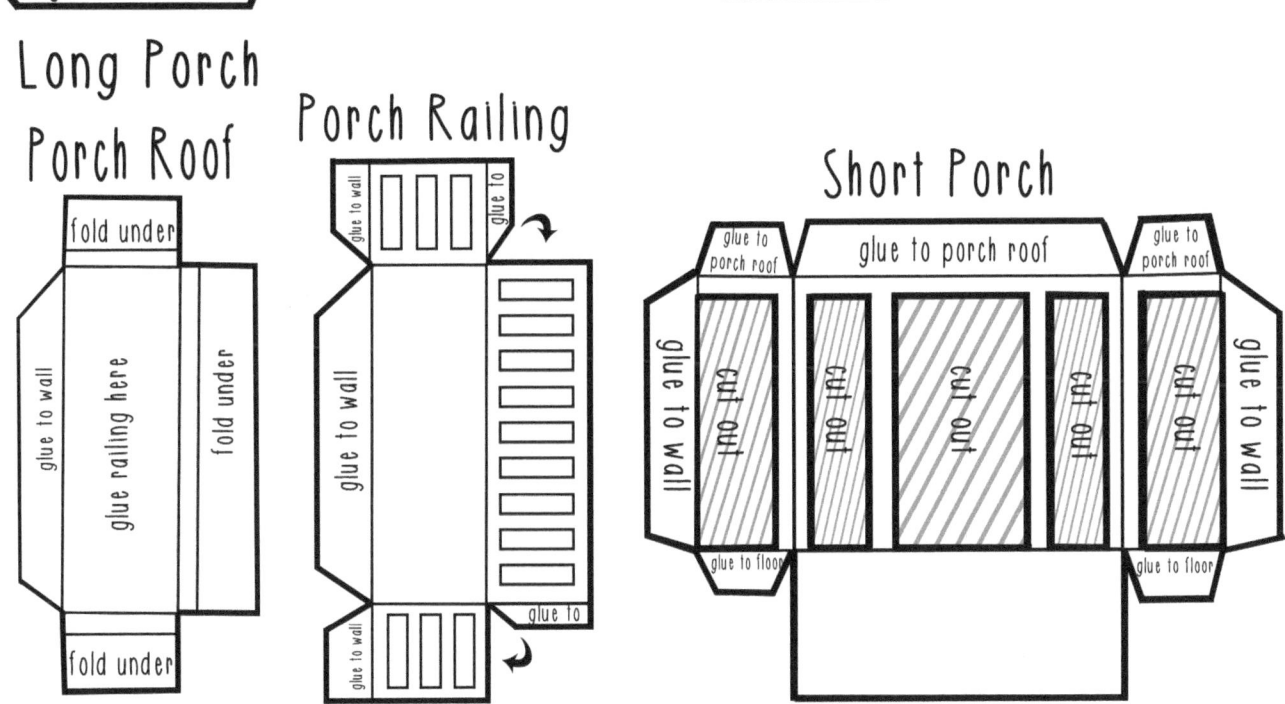

Nebraska Stone Farmhouse

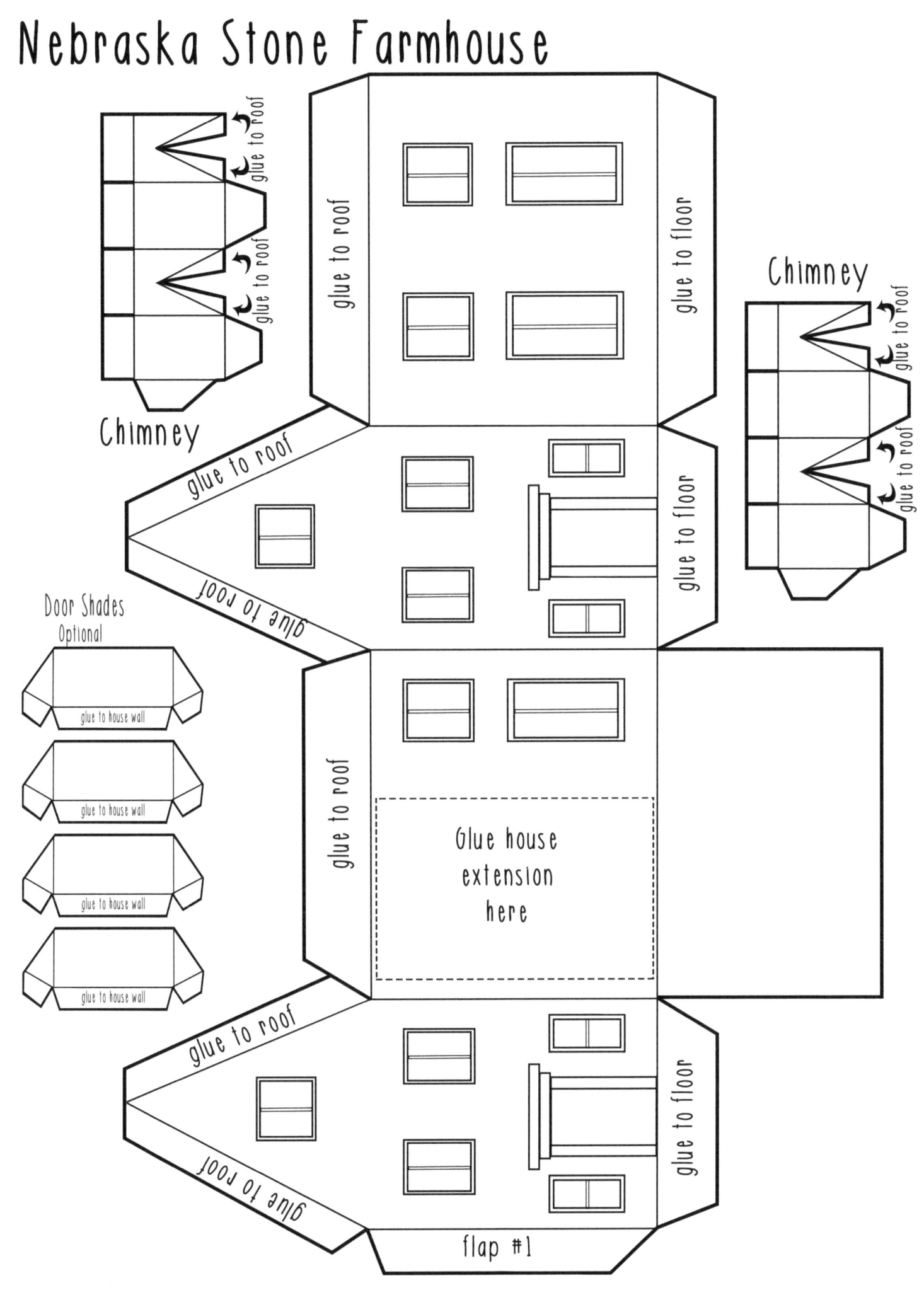

Nebraska Stone Farmhouse

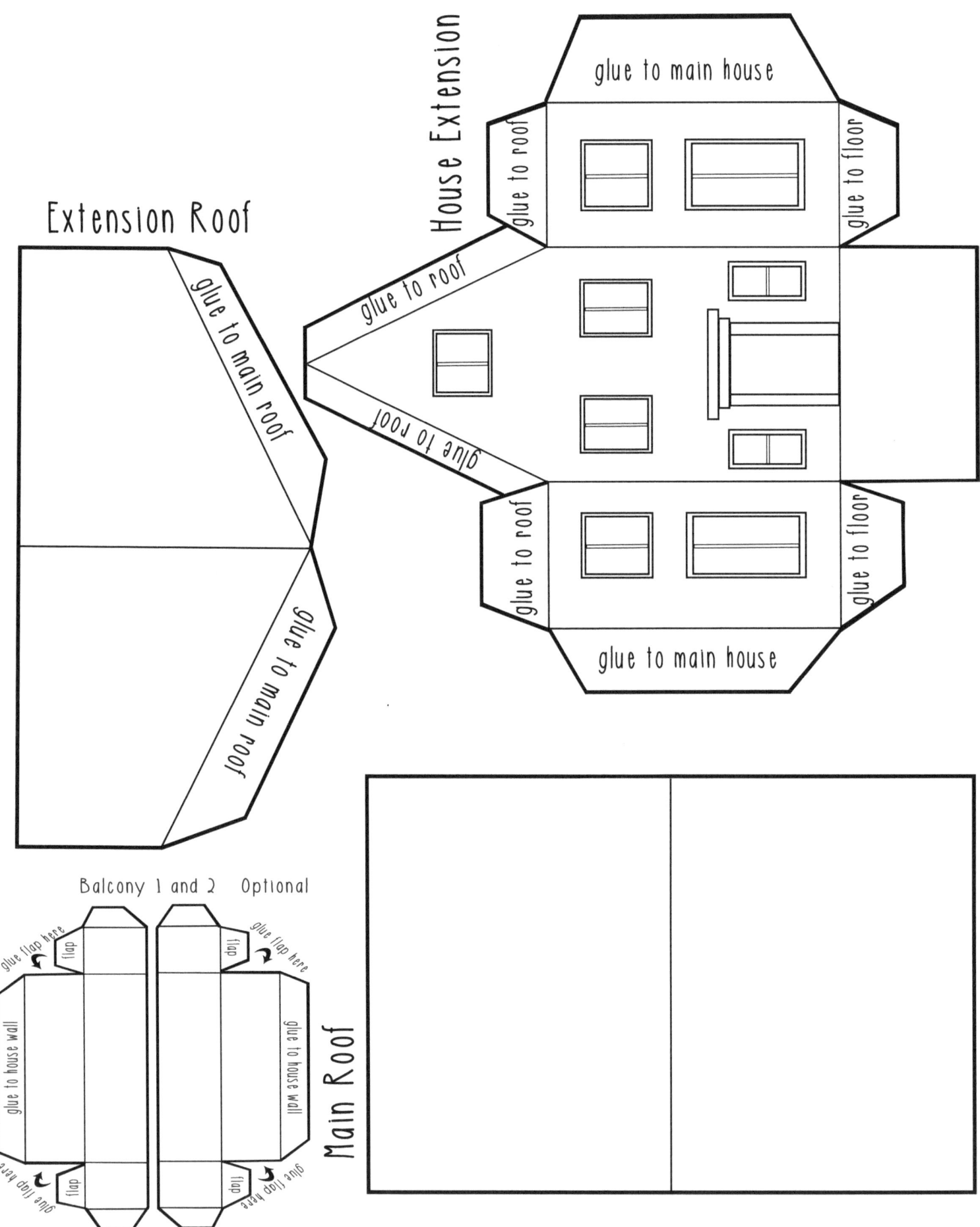

Nebraska Stone Farmhouse Construction

  The Nebraska Stone Farmhouse has several parts including chimneys and a house extension to be glued onto the main house building. There are balconies and door/window shades you can add or leave off. This is not a very complicated pattern and would be appropriate for students 1st grade and up. I even added an extra house extension on the other side of the main house for fun but isn't necessary. My children loved this one. The finished house measures about 5" x 4.5" x 4".

  Construction is done in the same way as the first chapter mentions. The pages are colored as you desire. The house parts are scored and glued first. The house extension building is glued together after the main building has the roof on. Next, glue the extension roof onto the house extension and the main roof. Next, glue the balcony and door shades if desired.

  The blank pattern without windows and doors are for creative students to add their own window and door designs.

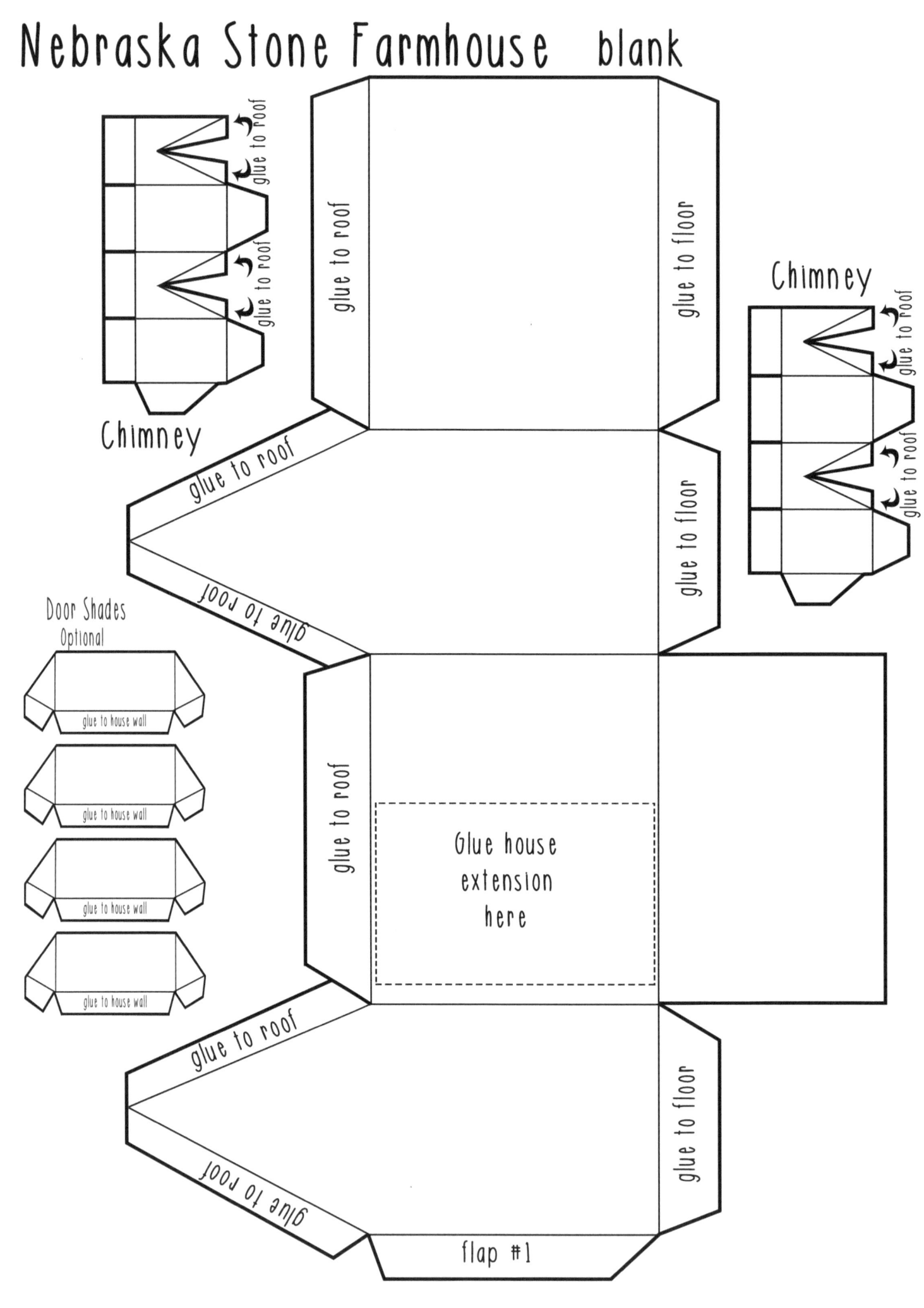

Nebraska Stone Farmhouse

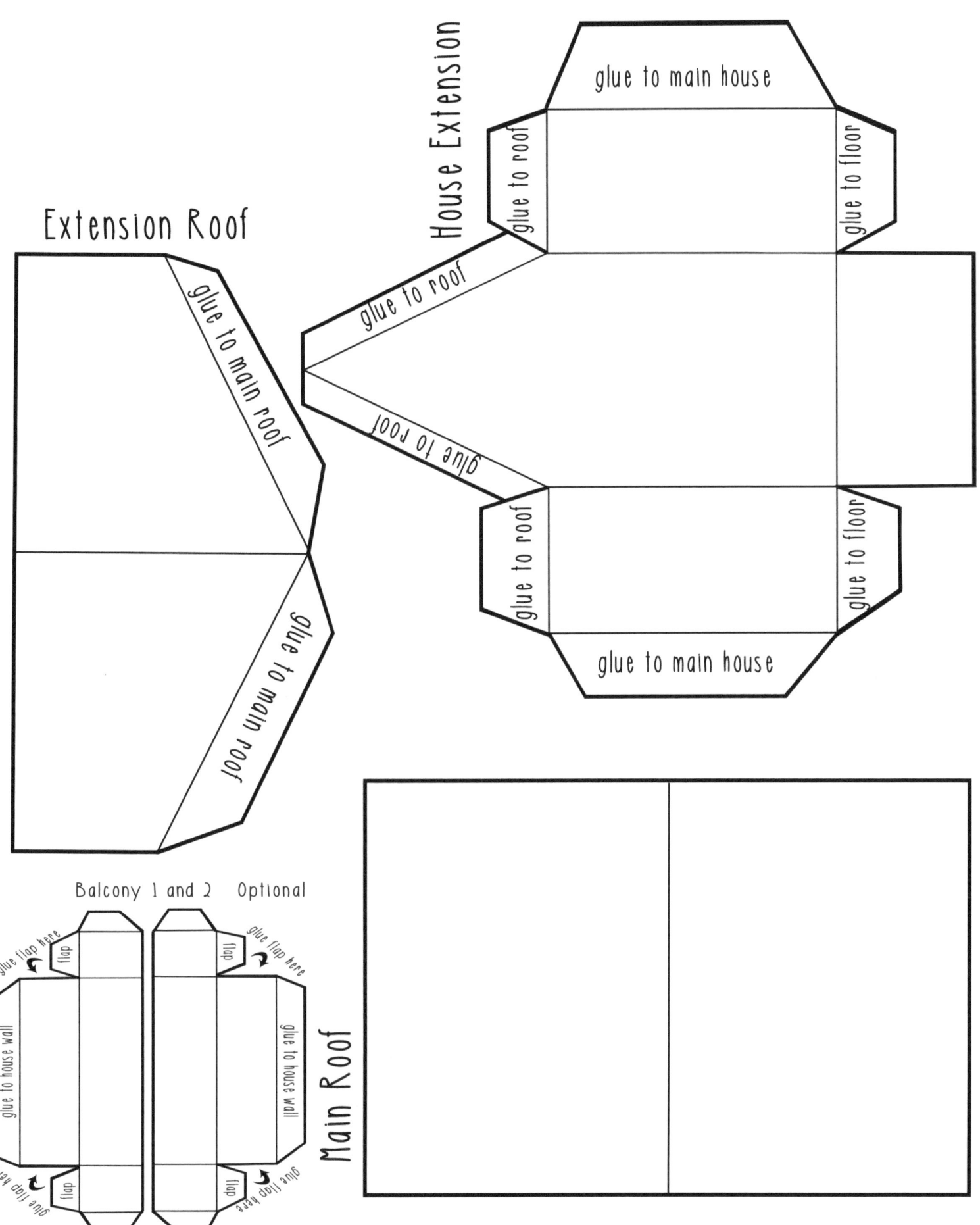

NORTH DAKOTA OLD RANCH HOUSE

North Dakota Ranch House

Main House

Chimney

Chimney

glue to roof
glue to roof
glue to floor
glue to roof
glue to roof
glue to floor
glue to roof
glue to roof
glue to floor

Glue Small House #1 Here

Glue Small House #2 Here

flap #1

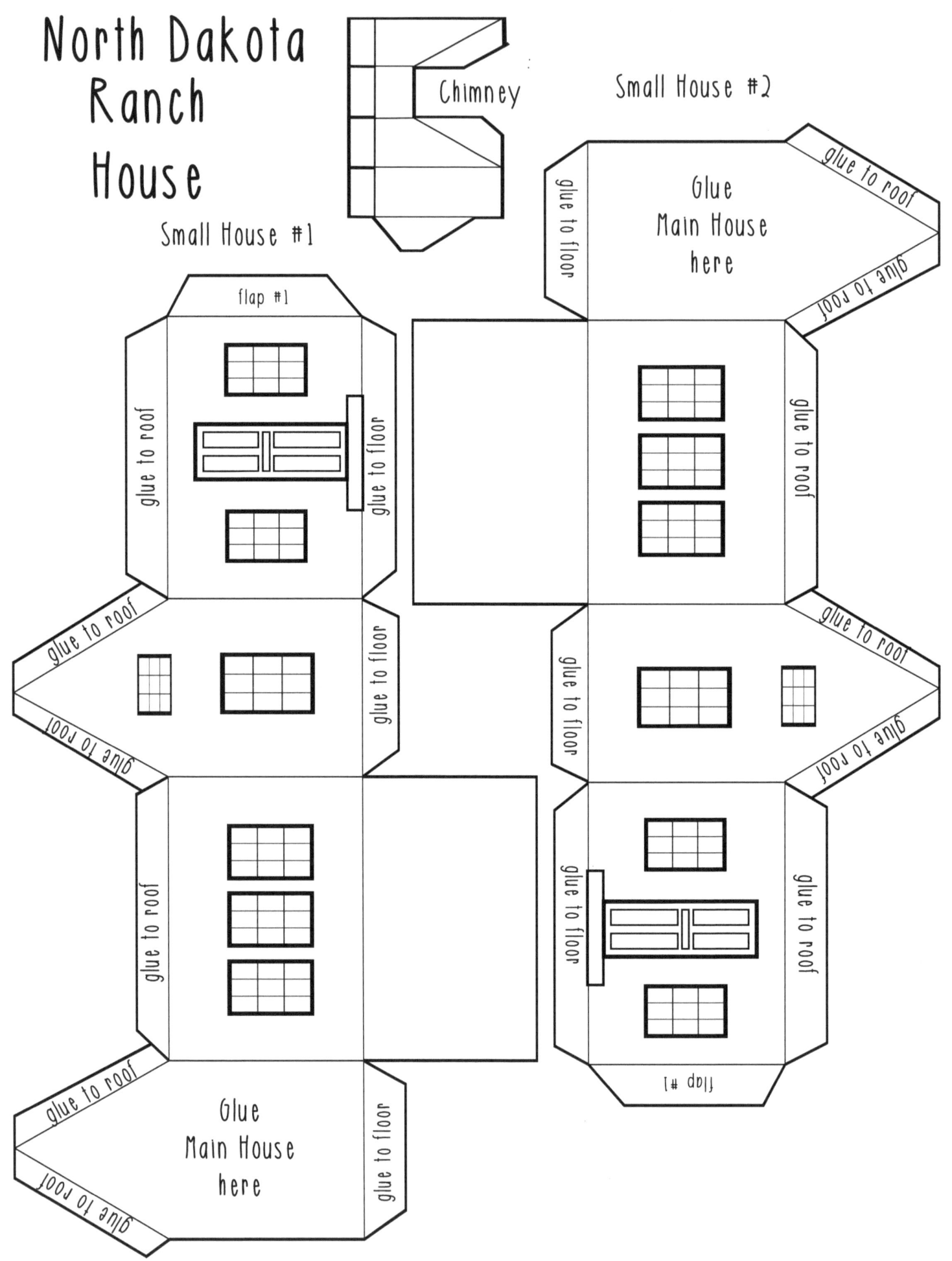

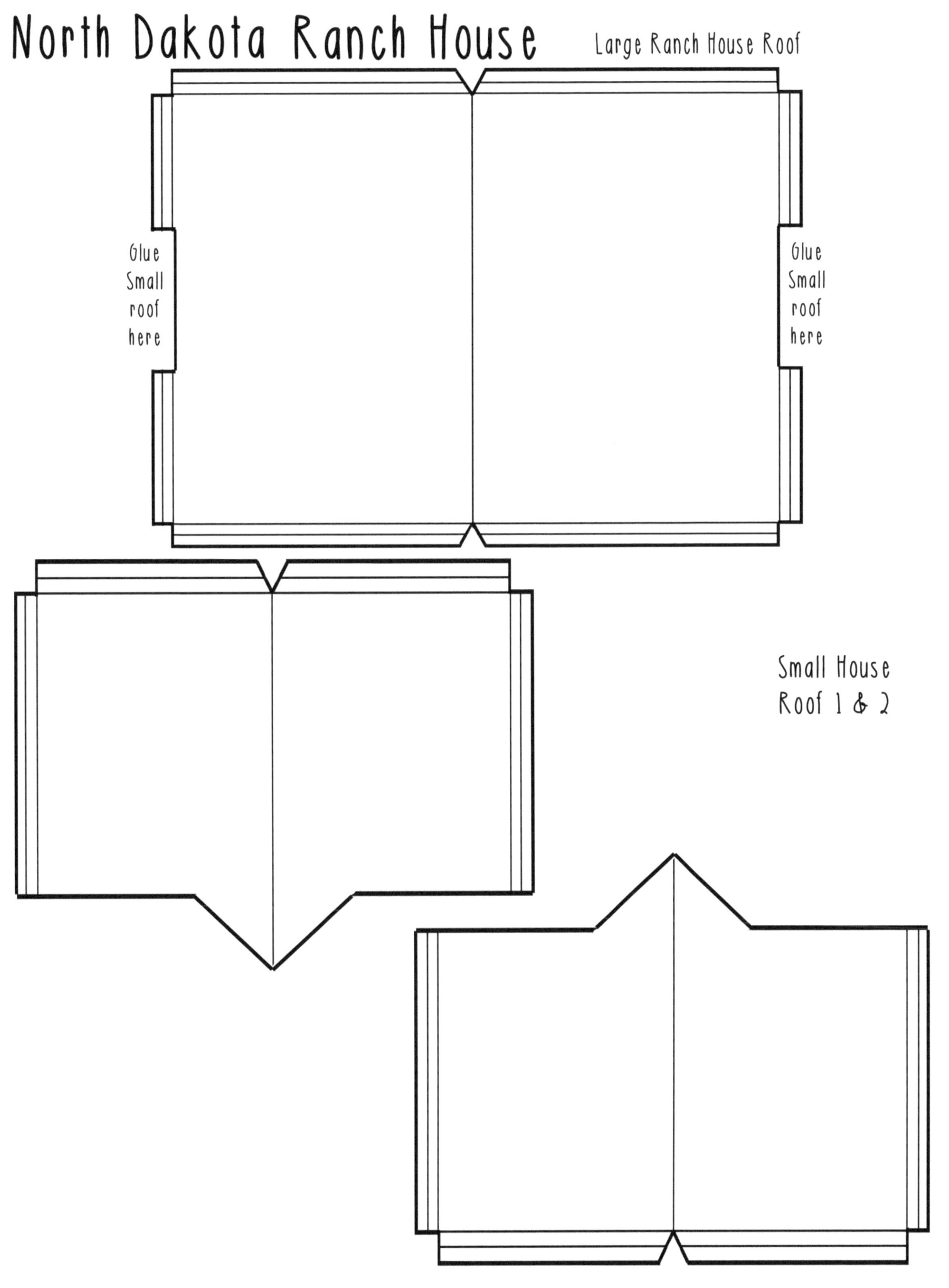

North Dakota Old Ranch House Construction

    This North Dakota Old Ranch House has a timber frame and a wood look so I colored mine brown. However any color you like is appropriate. The construction is three buildings glued together. I added some stacked and glued pieces of scrap paper to create the steps in front of the doors. This is optional but adds a little to the charm. I would say this is a good beginner to medium level of difficulty. Kindergarteners should leave off the chimneys as they are really the only difficult element. The finished house measures about 7" x 4.5" x 4".

    Construction is done in the same way as the first chapter mentions. The pages are colored as you desire. The main house is scored and glued first and the roof attached before the second and third buildings are glued together. It is a nice extra to add a paper bead or ball bead onto the door for a door knob.

    The chimneys are option and can be left off. Some patterns for other houses have window shades and balconies and although this pattern does not have any, you can use them here if you like for the back door or windows.

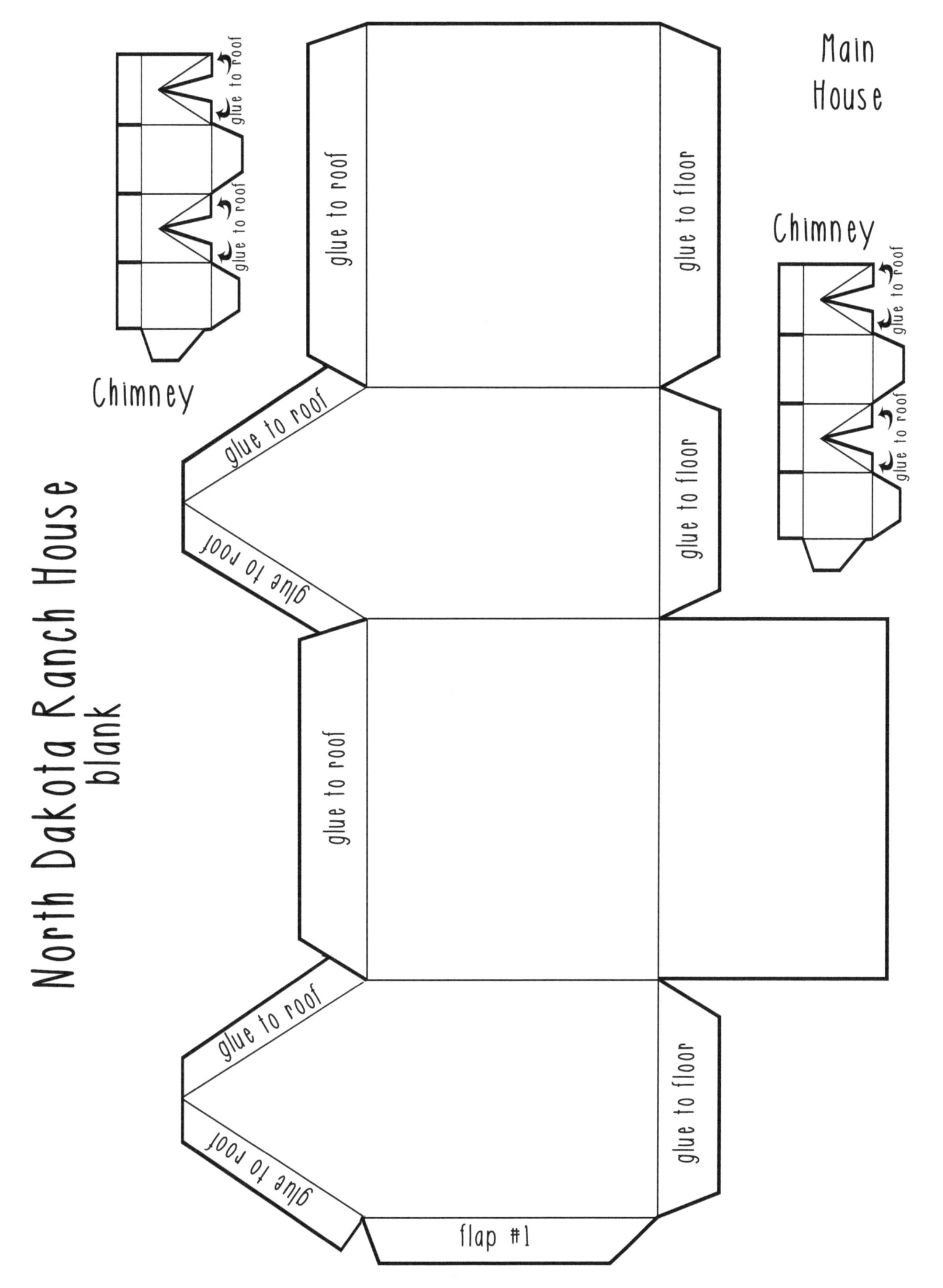

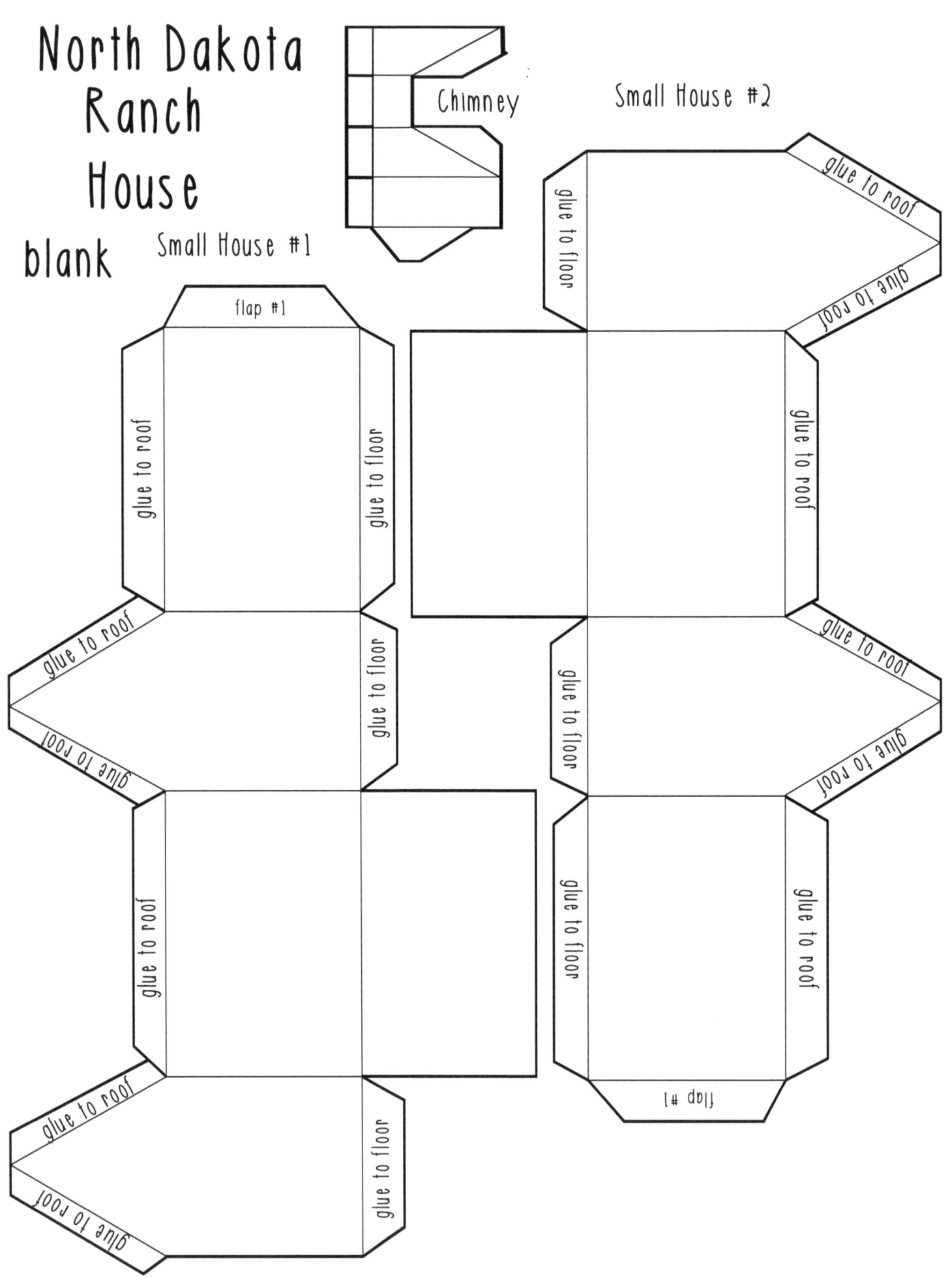

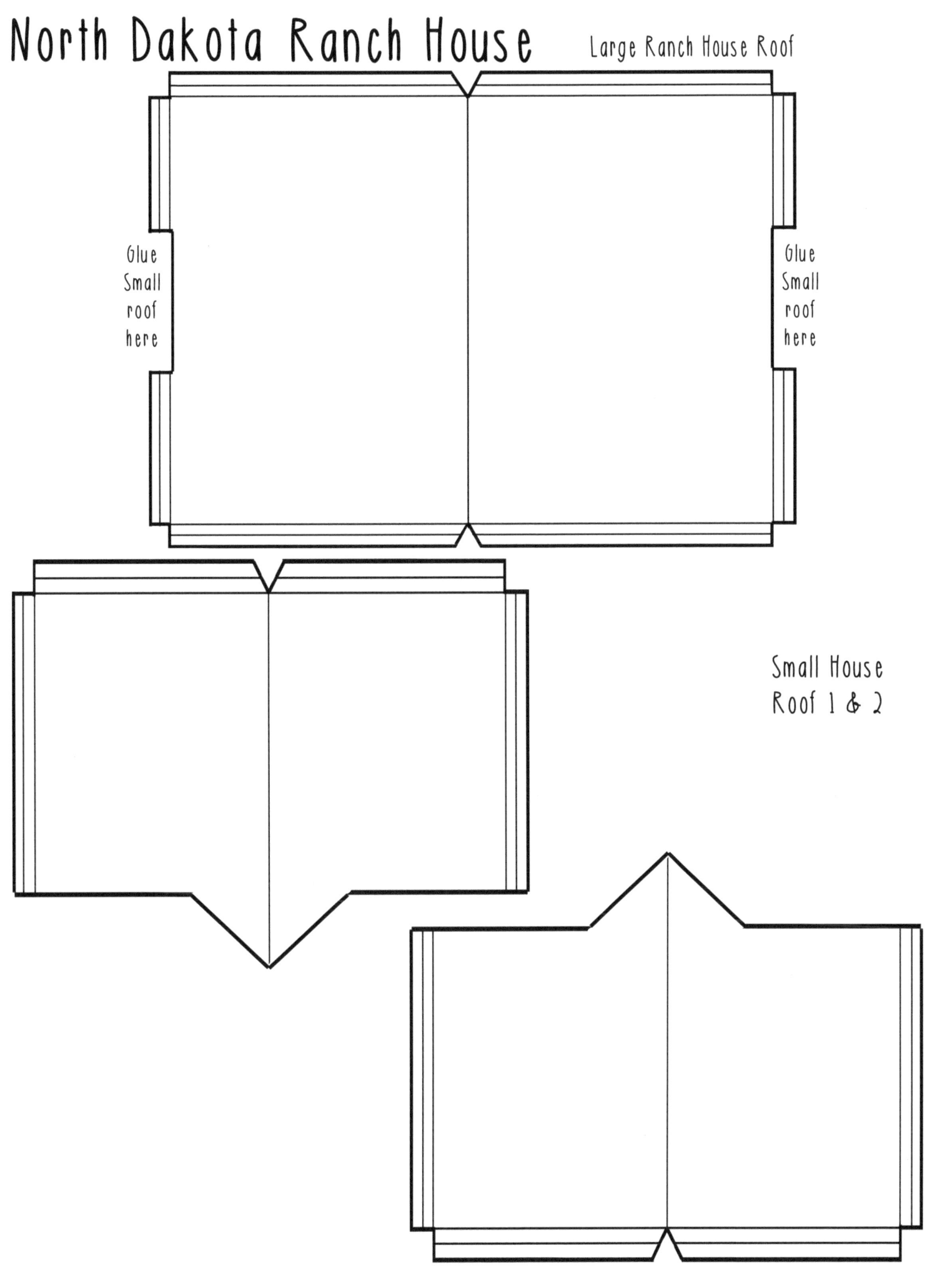

• • • TERMS OF USE • • •

By purchasing these files, you agree to the following terms:

These patterns are for personal and classroom use only. You may not sub-license, re-sell, share, claim as your own, otherwise distribute the graphics or resell them "as is" (whether digitally or physically).

You may positively print out these images and use them in your projects for sale. (for example: Christmas Villages, or other physical art work)

You may also resize these images to your liking.

***But, you agree NOT to digitally reproduce these images or print them out for sale in any form.

You may NOT use these images (altered or not) in your own digital work, collages or graphic designs in any form.

You also agree NOT to share or sell these images or use them for backgrounds in websites or claim them as your own work.

When you purchase these patterns, you are ONLY purchasing a license to use the patterns. Denise McGill and Dancing Paintbrush Co will retain full copyright on artwork and patterns.

Copyright 2019 by Denise McGill
Dancing Paintbrush Co
dancingpaintbrush@gmail.com
www.dancingpaintbrushco.com

All rights reserved. This book is for personal or classroom use and not to be resold in any manner either by electronic or mechanical reproduction, including photography, recording, or any information and retrieval system, all or in part except for the express use in educational classroom use or individual or by the express permission of the author.

ISBN 978-0-359-64189-5